Holding Needles and Yarn

Yarn may be placed over forefinger of either left hand or right hand. Hold yarn in the way you find easy and natural.

Holding yarn over forefinger of left hand

Holding yarn over forefinger of right hand

Casting on

Thumb method:

There are several methods for casting on and the following two methods are most frequently used. It is easy for a beginner to work and the cast-on stitches are neat and elastic.

① Hold yarn over forefinger.

Use needle 2 sizes larger.

② Leave shorter end 3 times as long as width of edge to be cast on. Hold shorter yarn over thumb.

Shorter end.

③

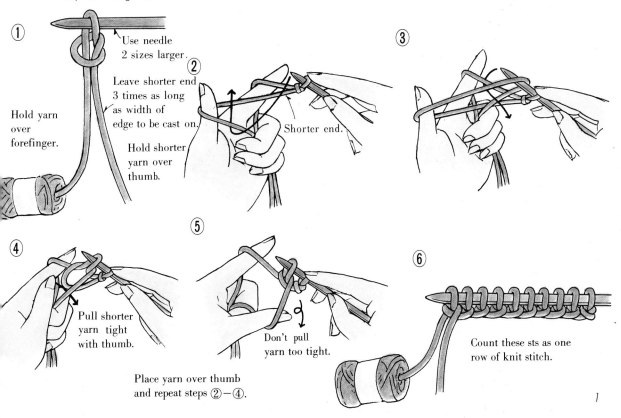

④ Pull shorter yarn tight with thumb.

⑤ Don't pull yarn too tight.

Place yarn over thumb and repeat steps ②—④.

⑥ Count these sts as one row of knit stitch.

1

Casting on through loops of chain :

Stitches are made through loops of chain which has been worked with contrasting color. The chain should be removed later. This method is suitable for edge of sleeve or body where ribbing is worked later.

① Make same number of foundation chain with casting-on stitches plus one or two sts using contrasting color.

Pick up back stitches of chain.

② Leave about 30cm.

Pick up stitches through loops with yarn to be used for the project.

③ Count as first row of right side.

④

Remove foundation chain and place stitches on needle.

Circular knitting :

Cast on required number of stitches with one needle in Thumb Method. Then divide cast-on stitches evenly among three needles or place them onto circular needle and work around. Circular knitting forms seamless and tubular fabrics, so it is suitable for making gloves, socks or small pieces. Remember you always face the right side of knitting when working in rounds.

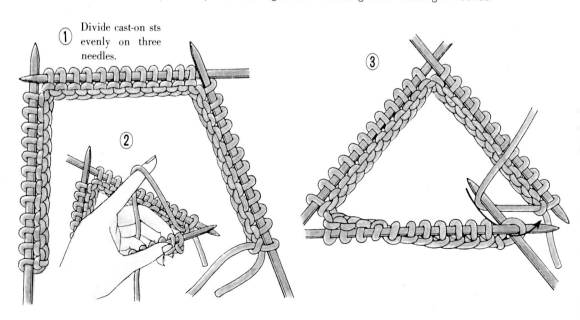

① Divide cast-on sts evenly on three needles.

②

③

Casting on stitches for K1, P1 rib.

This method forms the same edge worked in K1, P1 rib, so it is suitable for starting cap or front border. Also good for continuing to work in cable st and Aran pattern after ribbing.

Casting on sts for K1, P1 rib.:

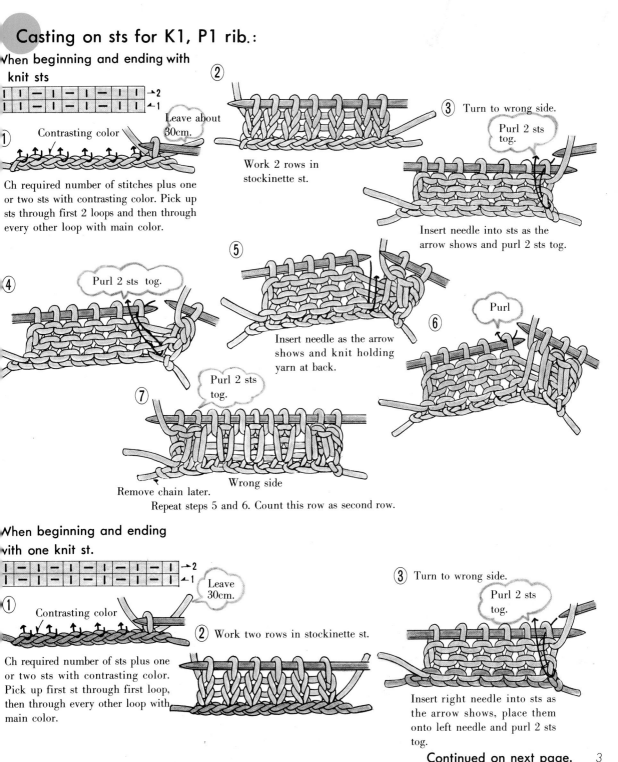

When beginning and ending with knit sts

→ 2
← 1

① Contrasting color

Leave about 30cm.

Ch required number of stitches plus one or two sts with contrasting color. Pick up sts through first 2 loops and then through every other loop with main color.

② Work 2 rows in stockinette st.

③ Turn to wrong side.
Purl 2 sts tog.

Insert needle into sts as the arrow shows and purl 2 sts tog.

④ Purl 2 sts tog.

⑤ Insert needle as the arrow shows and knit holding yarn at back.

⑥ Purl

⑦ Purl 2 sts tog.

Remove chain later.
Wrong side
Repeat steps 5 and 6. Count this row as second row.

When beginning and ending with one knit st.

→ 2
← 1

① Contrasting color

Leave 30cm.

Ch required number of sts plus one or two sts with contrasting color. Pick up first st through first loop, then through every other loop with main color.

② Work two rows in stockinette st.

③ Turn to wrong side.
Purl 2 sts tog.

Insert right needle into sts as the arrow shows, place them onto left needle and purl 2 sts tog.

Continued on next page.

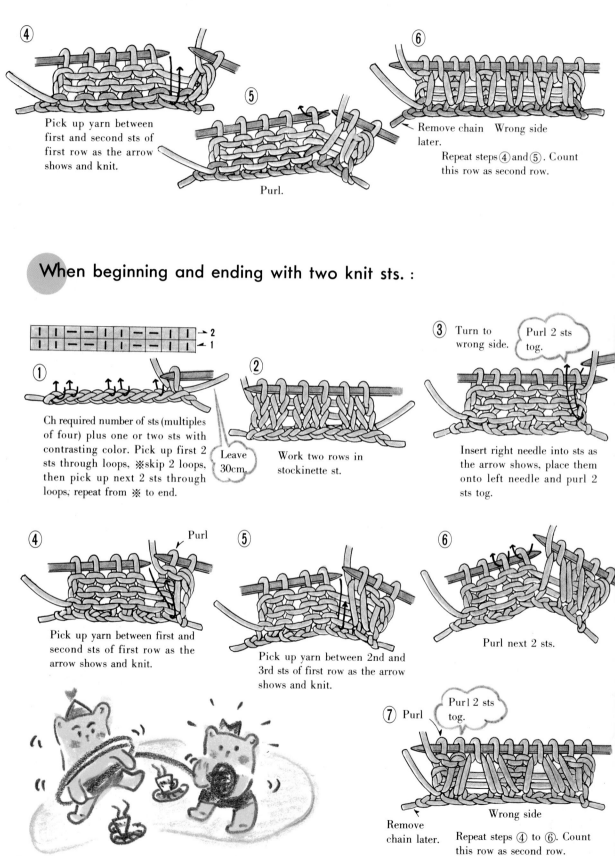

④ Pick up yarn between first and second sts of first row as the arrow shows and knit.

⑤ Purl.

⑥ ← Remove chain   Wrong side later.

Repeat steps④and⑤. Count this row as second row.

When beginning and ending with two knit sts. :

① Ch required number of sts (multiples of four) plus one or two sts with contrasting color. Pick up first 2 sts through loops, ※skip 2 loops, then pick up next 2 sts through loops; repeat from ※ to end.

Leave 30cm.

② Work two rows in stockinette st.

③ Turn to wrong side.

Purl 2 sts tog.

Insert right needle into sts as the arrow shows, place them onto left needle and purl 2 sts tog.

④ Purl

Pick up yarn between first and second sts of first row as the arrow shows and knit.

⑤ Pick up yarn between 2nd and 3rd sts of first row as the arrow shows and knit.

⑥ Purl next 2 sts.

⑦ Purl

Purl 2 sts tog.

Remove chain later.

Wrong side

Repeat steps ④ to ⑥. Count this row as second row.

Stitch Key to Knitting

The chart shows only right side of knitting. Learn stitch symbols and the right way to knit following diagrams.

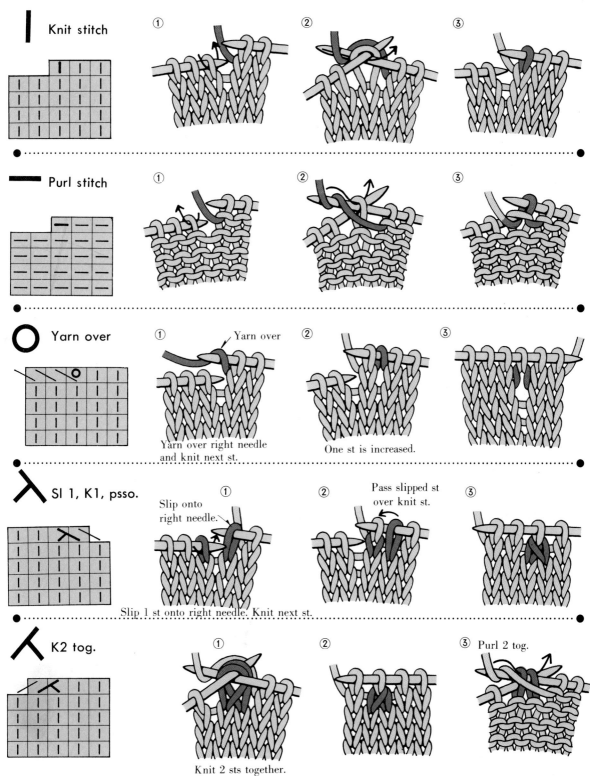

| Knit stitch

① ② ③

▬ Purl stitch

① ② ③

O Yarn over

① Yarn over ② ③

Yarn over right needle and knit next st.

One st is increased.

⅄ Sl 1, K1, psso.

Slip onto right needle. ① ② Pass slipped st over knit st. ③

Slip 1 st onto right needle. Knit next st.

⅄ K2 tog.

① ② ③ Purl 2 tog.

Knit 2 sts together.

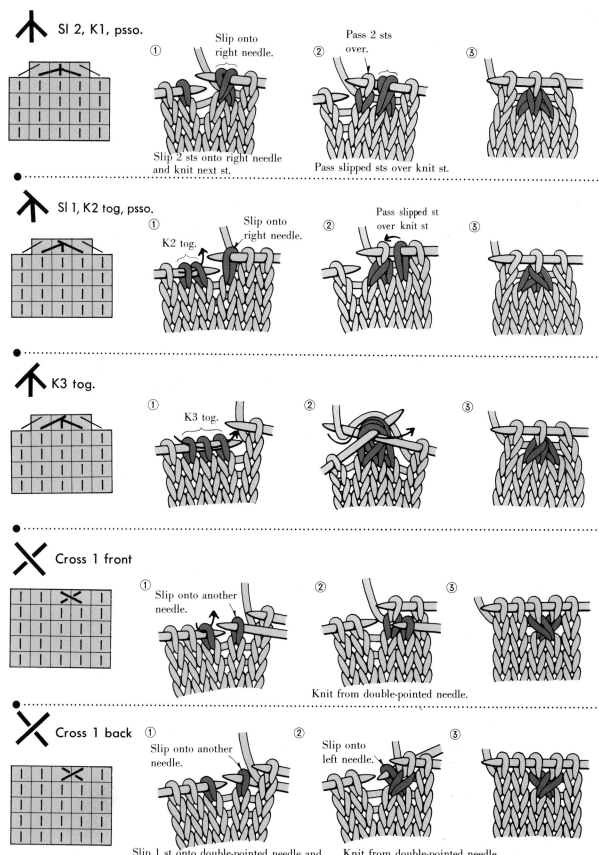

Sl 2, K1, psso.

① Slip onto right needle.
Slip 2 sts onto right needle and knit next st.

② Pass 2 sts over.
Pass slipped sts over knit st.

③

Sl 1, K2 tog, psso.

① K2 tog. Slip onto right needle.

② Pass slipped st over knit st

③

K3 tog.

① K3 tog.

②

③

Cross 1 front

① Slip onto another needle.

②

③
Knit from double-pointed needle.

Cross 1 back

① Slip onto another needle.

② Slip onto left needle.

③

Slip 1 st onto double-pointed needle and hold at back of work. Knit next st.

Knit from double-pointed needle.

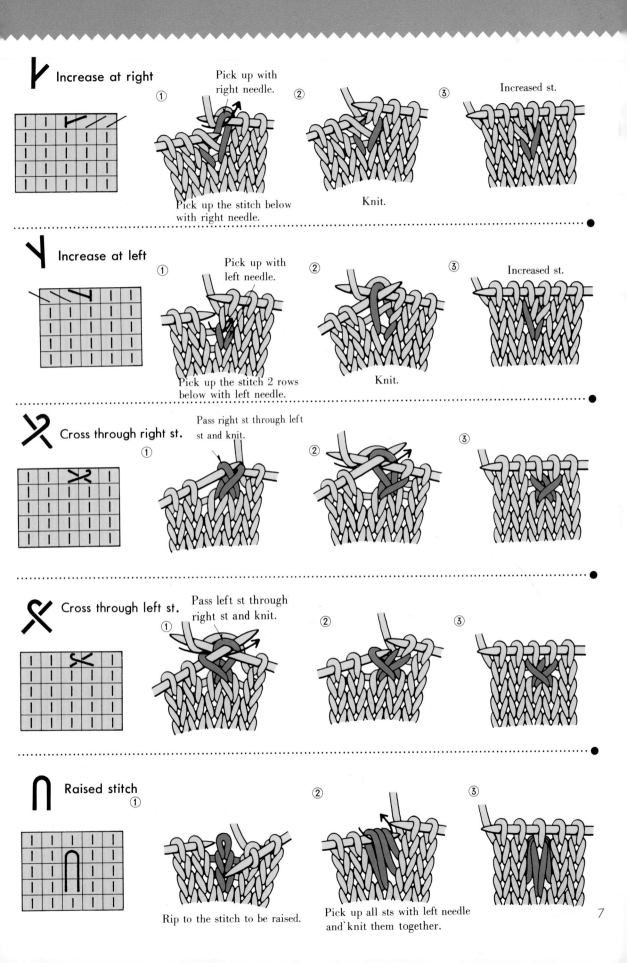

Increase at right

① Pick up with right needle.

Pick up the stitch below with right needle.

② Knit.

③ Increased st.

Increase at left

① Pick up with left needle.

Pick up the stitch 2 rows below with left needle.

② Knit.

③ Increased st.

Cross through right st.

Pass right st through left st and knit.

① ② ③

Cross through left st.

Pass left st through right st and knit.

① ② ③

Raised stitch

① Rip to the stitch to be raised.

② Pick up all sts with left needle and knit them together.

③

7

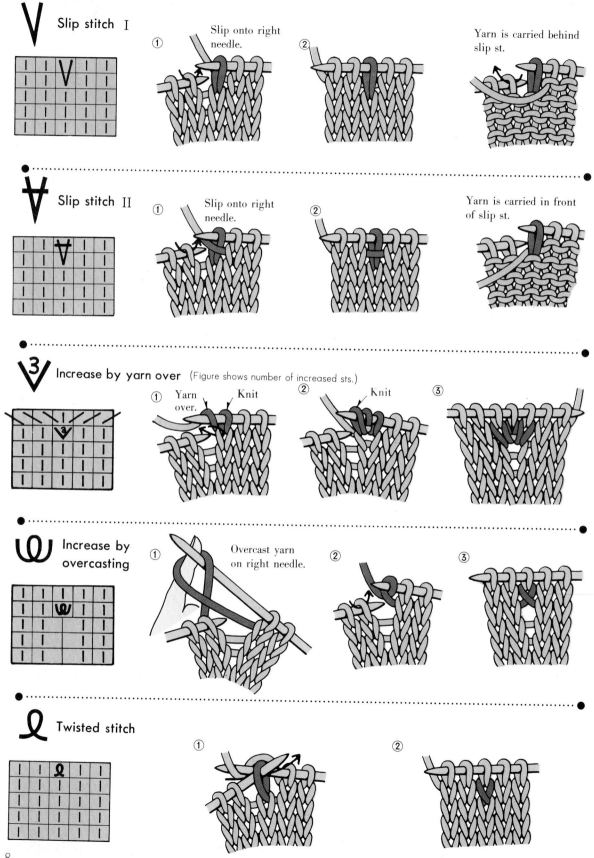

V — Slip stitch I

① Slip onto right needle.

②

Yarn is carried behind slip st.

∀ — Slip stitch II

① Slip onto right needle.

②

Yarn is carried in front of slip st.

⅋ — Increase by yarn over (Figure shows number of increased sts.)

① Yarn over. Knit

② Knit

③

ɯ — Increase by overcasting

① Overcast yarn on right needle.

②

③

ℓ — Twisted stitch

①

②

8

Decreasing

To decrease one st at the beginning of row:

For the right side

① Slip first st onto right needle. Knit next st.

② Pass slipped st over knit st.

③

④

LEFT EDGE

RIGHT EDGE

For the left side

① Knit to last 2 sts. Then knit 2 sts together.

②

③

To decrease second stitch from edge:

For the right side

① Knit first st, slip second st. Knit 3rd st and pass slipped st over 3rd st.

② Knit next st.

③

For the left side

①

②

③

Knit to last 3 sts.

Then knit 2 sts together.

Knit last st.

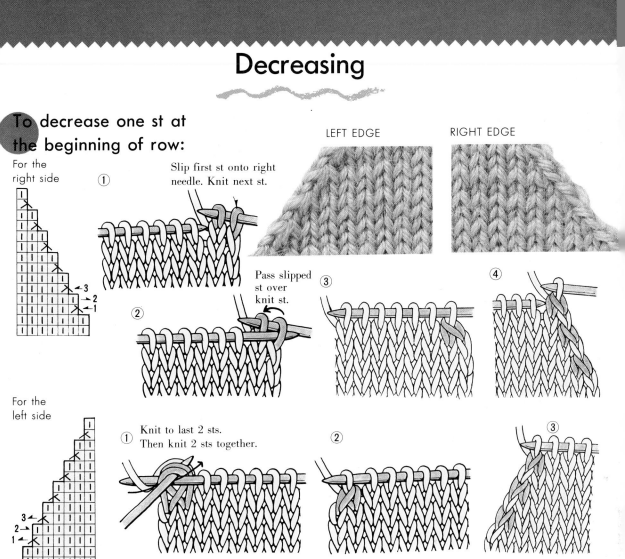
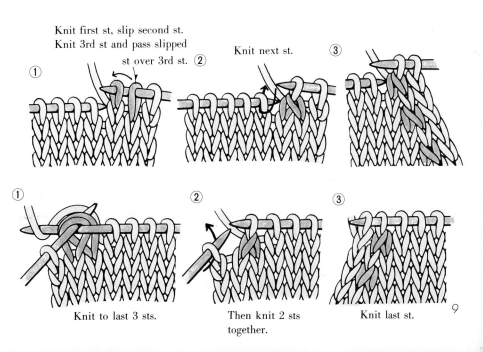
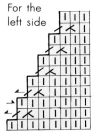
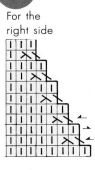

Shaping armholes:

Shaping armholes at right angles

6 sts. Stockinette st. 6 sts.

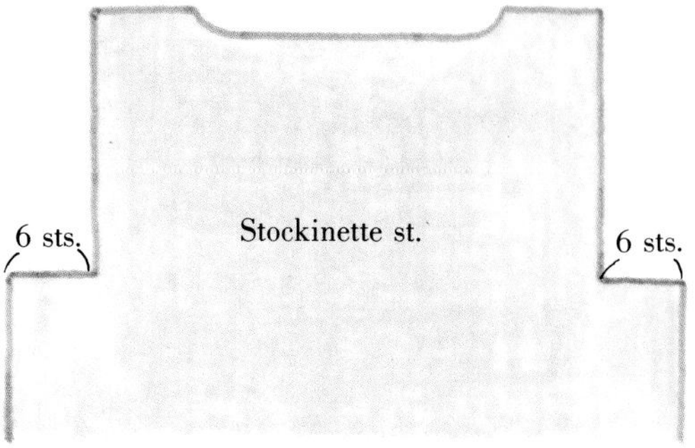

There are two methods for shaping armholes at right angles; one is to bind off sts to be decreased and the other is to hold them on a holder. Sleeve can be joined to body with crocheted slip st or with grafting method. When armholes are shaped by bound-off method, it may be easier to join the sleeves, but seam becomes a bit cumbersome. On the other hand, when extra stitches are hold on a holder, they will be grafted with sleeves. Grafting method is suitable when yarn is thick.

Binding off

For right armhole

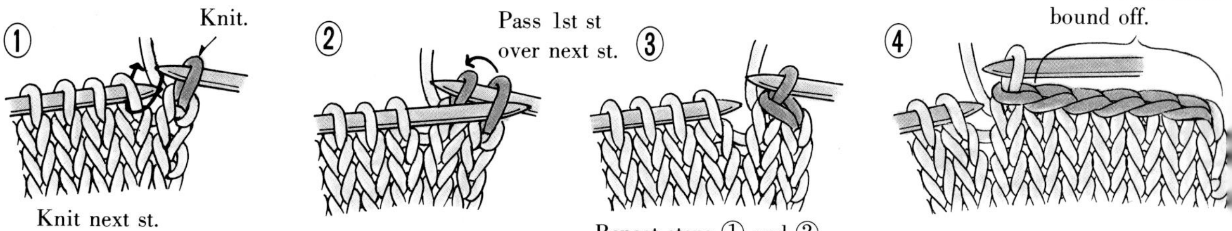

① Knit.
Knit next st.

② Pass 1st st over next st. ③

Repeat steps ① and ②.

④ Six sts have been bound off.

For left armhole

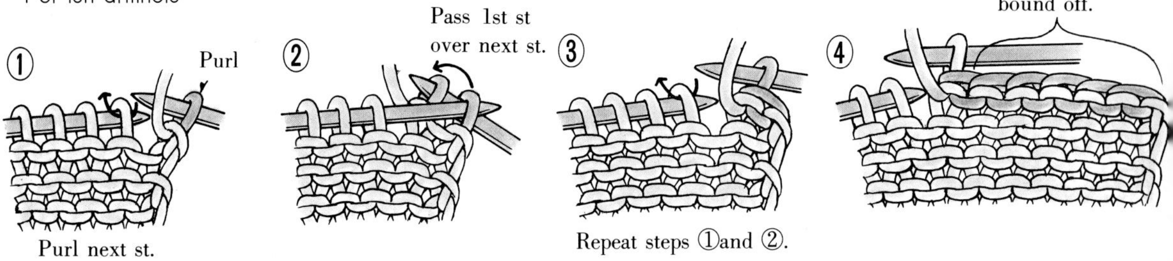

① Purl
Purl next st.

② Pass 1st st over next st. ③

Repeat steps ① and ②.

④ Six sts have been bound off.

For left armhole
Six sts bound off.
2
1
78

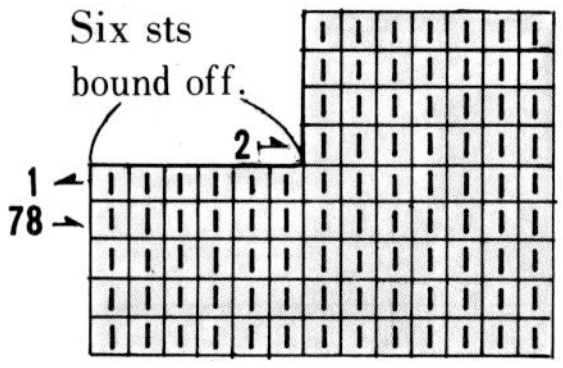

Starting at right side, bind off 6 sts and knit to end. Turn to wrong side, bind off 6 sts and purl to end. Turn and work even until required length is reached.

For right armhole
Six sts bound off.
2
1
78

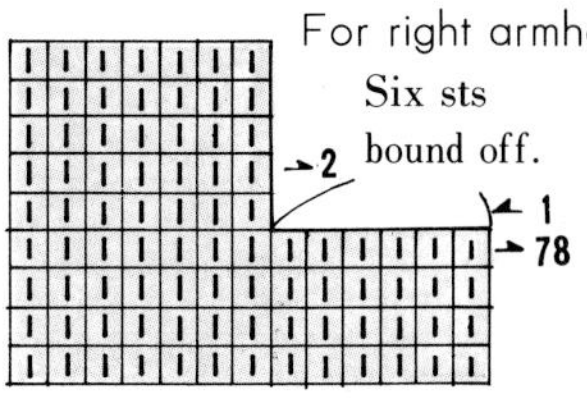

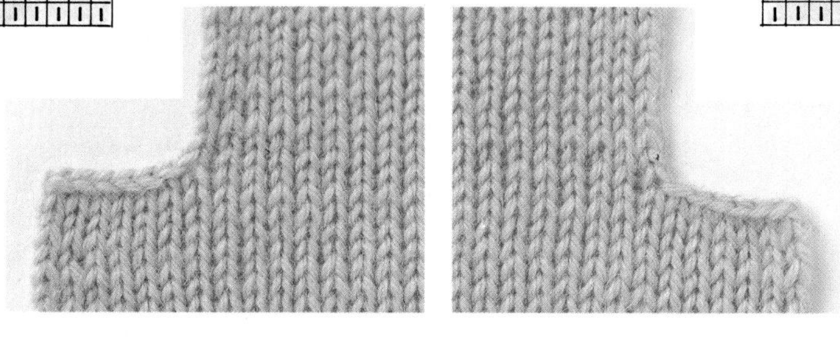

Holding

Left armhole

Work first row of armholes with wrong side facing to last 6 sts. Place these 6 sts onto a holder. Work 2nd row to last 6 sts and place them onto holder as for first row. Work even from 3rd row to shaping of neck.

Right armhole

Hold 6 sts.

2◄

1→
79◄

Hold 6 sts.

◄2
◄1
◄79

Shaping armholes along curved line

Stockinette st.

Bind off 4 sts once,
3 sts every other row once,
dec 1st each row twice,
every other row once.

Remember that decreasing starts at first row of armhole on right side and at second row on left side. Thus there is one row difference between right and left sides (see chart below).

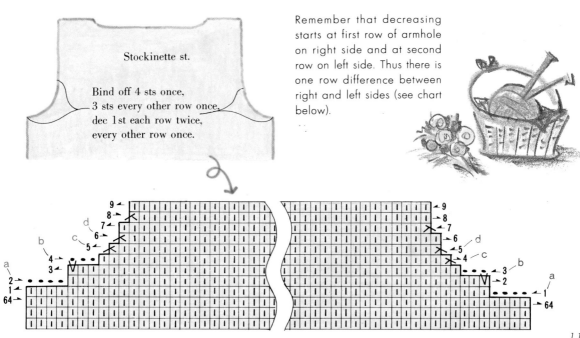

Shaping right armhole

Decreasing more than 2 stitches

To angle the corner (first row).

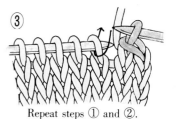

① Knit next st. ← Knit

② Pass first st over second st.

③ Repeat steps ① and ②.

To decrease without angling (third row).

① Slip first st onto right needle.

② Pass first st over second st.

③ Repeat steps ① and ②.

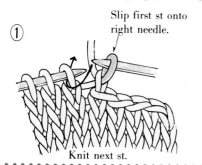

Knit next st.

Repeat steps ① and ②.

Decreasing one stitch

Purl 2 sts tog. (4th row).

(Work with wrong side facing)

① Draw needle off last 2 sts and insert needle into same sts, changing position of sts.

② Purl 2 sts tog.

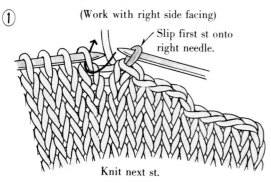

Sl 1, K1, psso (5th row).

① (Work with right side facing)

Slip first st onto right needle.

Knit next st.

② Pass slipped st over knit st.

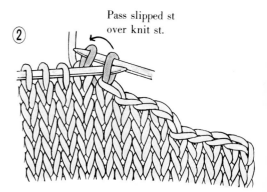

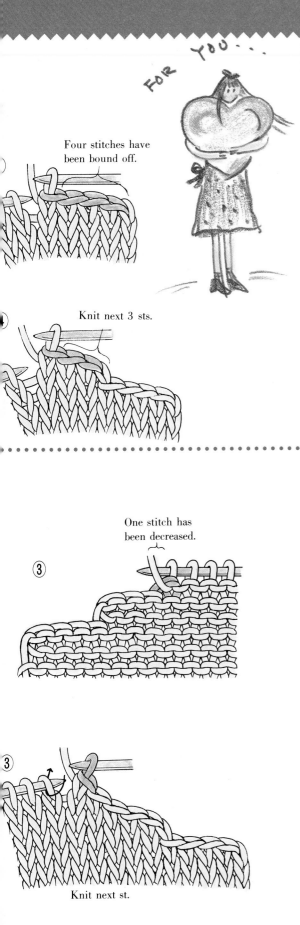

Four stitches have been bound off.

Knit next 3 sts.

One stitch has been decreased.

③

③

Knit next st.

Bind off 4 sts on first row angling the corner and 3 sts on third row without angling the corner; slip first st, knit next st and pass slipped st over knit st.

Right armhole

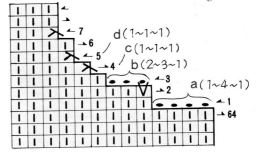

d (1~1~1)
c (1~1~1)
b (2~3~1)
a (1~4~1)

Shaping right armhole

Row 1: Knit first 2 sts, pass first st over second st.
Knit 3rd st and pass 2nd st over 3rd st.
Knit 4th st and pass 3rd st over 4th st.
Knit 5th st and pass 4th st over 5th st.
Four sts have been bound off.
Knit to end.

Row 2: Turn. Bind off 4 sts and purl to end (see next page).

Row 3: Turn. Slip first st, knit next st and pass slipped st over knit st.
Knit 3rd st and pass 2nd st over 3rd st.
Knit 4th st and pass 3rd st over 4th st.
Three sts have been bound off.
Knit to end.

Row 4: Turn. Bind off 3 sts (see next page) and purl to last 2 sts. Purl 2 sts tog.

Row 5: Turn. Sl 1, K1, psso.
Knit to last 2 sts and K2 tog (see next page).

Row 6: Turn. P2 tog (see next page) and purl to end.

Row 7: Turn. Sl 1, K1, psso. Knit to end.
From Row 8, work even. (On left side of Row 8, purl 2 sts tog and purl to end.)

Shaping left armhole

Decreasing more than 2 sts.

To angle the corner (2nd row).

① Purl next st.   Purl

② Pass first st over second one.

③ Repeat steps ① and ②.

To decrease without angling (4th row).

① Slip first st onto right needle.

Purl next st.

② Pass first st over second one.

③ Repeat steps ① and ②.

Decreasing one stitch

Knit 2 sts together (5th row).

Work with right side facing.

Insert needle into 2 sts.

② Knit 2 sts tog.

Knit 2 sts together (6th row).

Work with wrong side facing.

① Purl 2 sts tog.

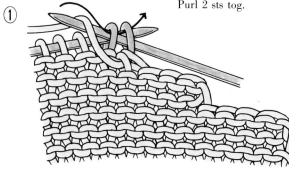

②

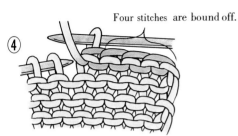

Four stitches are bound off.

④

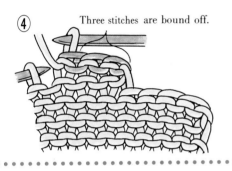

④ Three stitches are bound off.

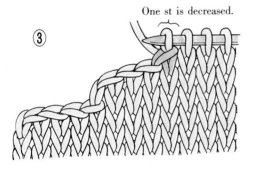

③ One st is decreased.

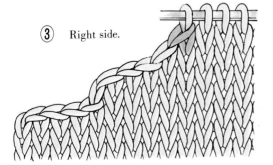

③ Right side.

Left armhole

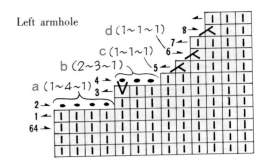

d (1~1~1)   8
c (1~1~1)   7   6
b (2~3~1)   5
a (1~4~1)   4
            3
2
1
64

Shaping left armhole

Row 1 : (Work with right side facing) Bind off 4 sts and knit to end.

Row 2 : Turn. Purl 2 sts, pass first st over second st.
Purl 3rd st and pass 2nd st over 3rd st.
Purl 4th st and pass 3rd st over 4th st.
Purl 5th st and pass 4th st over 5th st.
Four sts have been bound off. Purl to end.

Row 3 : Turn. Bind off 3 sts (see page 13) and knit to end.

Row 4 : Turn. Slip first st onto right needle, purl next st and pass slipped st over purl st.
Purl 3rd st and pass 2nd st over 3rd st.
Purl 4th st and pass 3rd st over 4th st.
Three sts have been bound off.
Purl to last 2 sts.
Purl 2 sts tog (see page 13).

Row 5 : Turn. Sl 1, K1, psso (see page 13) knit to last 2 sts, K2 tog.

Row 6 : Turn. Sl 1, P1, psso, purl to end.

Row 7 : Turn. Sl 1, K1, psso (see page 13), knit to end.

Row 8 : Turn. Sl 1, P1, psso, purl to end.
From Row 9, work even.

Increasing

Increasing one st.:

For easier and neater seams, increase one st between first and second sts from the edge.
Following are methods two often used.

Increasing one st from raised st

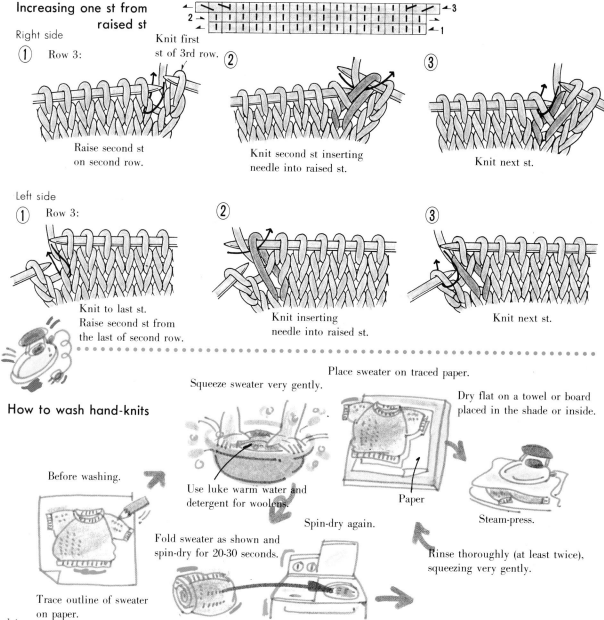

Right side

① Row 3:

Knit first st of 3rd row.

Raise second st on second row.

② Knit second st inserting needle into raised st.

③ Knit next st.

Left side

① Row 3:

Knit to last st. Raise second st from the last of second row.

② Knit inserting needle into raised st.

③ Knit next st.

How to wash hand-knits

Before washing.

Trace outline of sweater on paper.

Use luke warm water and detergent for woolens.

Squeeze sweater very gently.

Fold sweater as shown and spin-dry for 20-30 seconds.

Spin-dry again.

Rinse thoroughly (at least twice), squeezing very gently.

Place sweater on traced paper.

Paper

Dry flat on a towel or board placed in the shade or inside.

Steam-press.

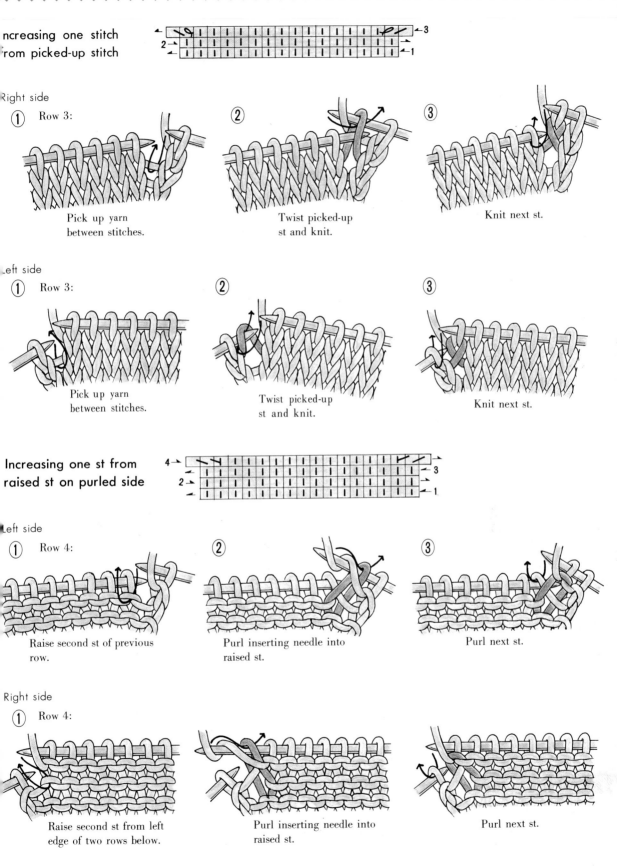

Increasing one stitch from picked-up stitch

Right side

① Row 3:

Pick up yarn between stitches.

②

Twist picked-up st and knit.

③

Knit next st.

Left side

① Row 3:

Pick up yarn between stitches.

②

Twist picked-up st and knit.

③

Knit next st.

Increasing one st from raised st on purled side

Left side

① Row 4:

Raise second st of previous row.

②

Purl inserting needle into raised st.

③

Purl next st.

Right side

① Row 4:

Raise second st from left edge of two rows below.

②

Purl inserting needle into raised st.

③

Purl next st.

Increasing more than 2 stitches on the edge(by overcasting):

Increase required number of sts for underarms of French or dolman sleeves by overcasting. This method is suitable for increasing along curved line. Overcast sts are not counted as one row. Slip first st on each row for a neater finish.

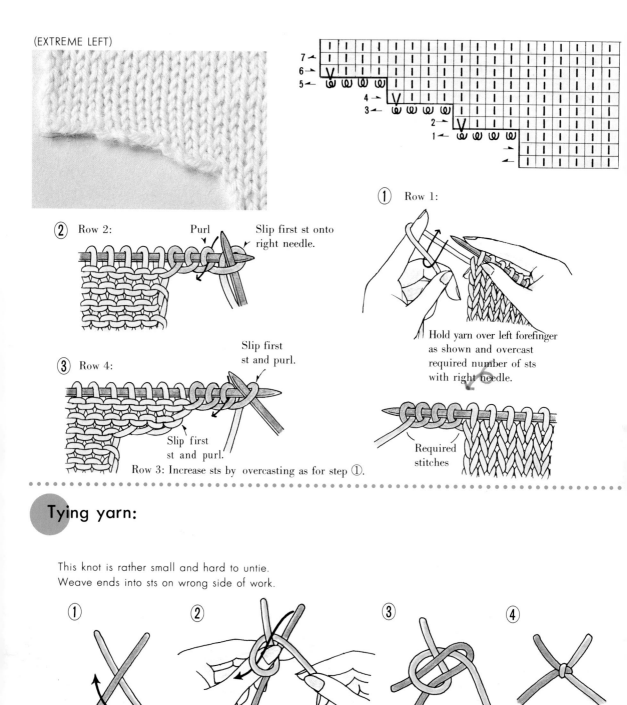

(EXTREME LEFT)

① Row 1:

Hold yarn over left forefinger as shown and overcast required number of sts with right needle.

Required stitches

② Row 2:   Purl   Slip first st onto right needle.

③ Row 4:

Slip first st and purl.

Slip first st and purl.

Row 3: Increase sts by overcasting as for step ①.

Tying yarn:

This knot is rather small and hard to untie.
Weave ends into sts on wrong side of work.

① ② ③ ④

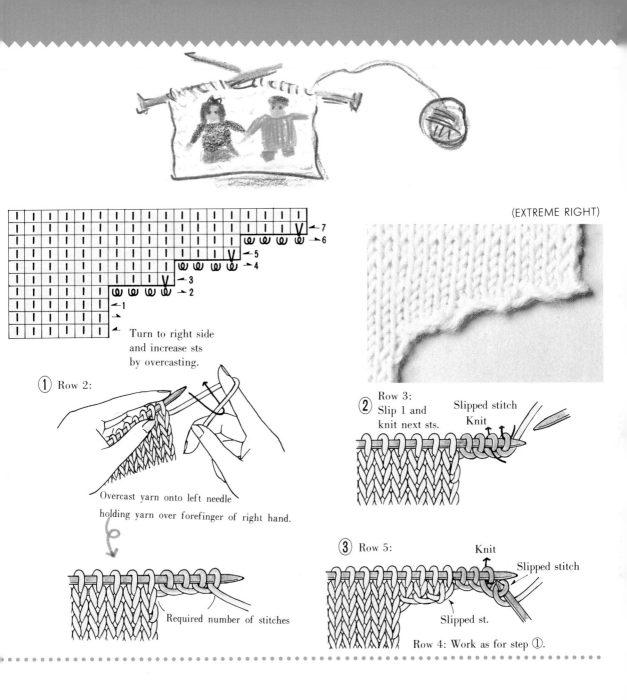

(EXTREME RIGHT)

Turn to right side
and increase sts
by overcasting.

① Row 2:

Overcast yarn onto left needle
holding yarn over forefinger of right hand.

Required number of stitches

② Row 3:
Slip 1 and
knit next sts.

Slipped stitch
Knit

③ Row 5:

Knit

Slipped stitch

Slipped st.

Row 4: Work as for step ①.

Joining new ball of yarn in the middle of row.

Leave 6-7cm end of old ball of yarn and work next st with new ball leaving 6-7cm end.
After finishing the piece, weave each end into sts on wrong side.

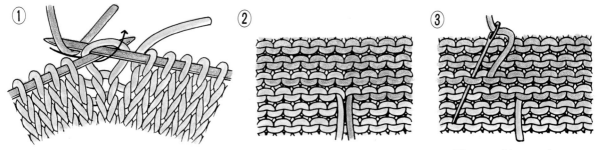

① ② ③

Weave end into work.

19

Shaping Shoulders

Shaping shoulders without binding off:

- Instead of binding off stitches to shape shoulders, decrease stitches as shown below leaving indicated sts on left needle.
- Decreasing for shaping right shoulder starts on first row and for left shoulder on second row, thus there is one row difference.
- Work finishing row to avoid making holes caused by slipped sts unless otherwise indicated.
  Finishing row is sometimes omitted when striped pattern or lacework is used.
  Shape shoulders following chart as shown below.

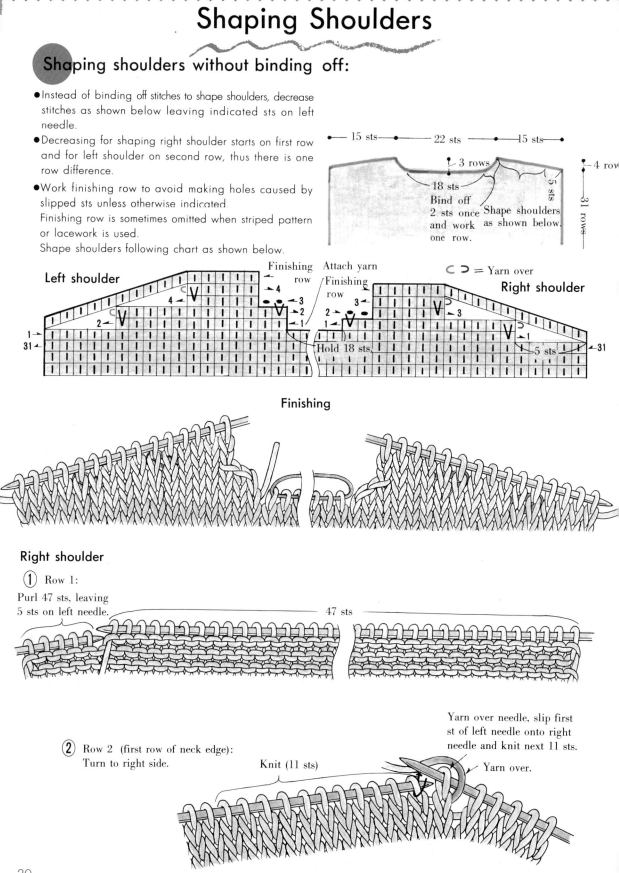

━ 15 sts ━ 22 sts ━ 15 sts ━

3 rows

18 sts
Bind off
2 sts once
and work
one row.

Shape shoulders
as shown below.

5 sts

4 row

31 rows

Left shoulder

⊂ ⊃ = Yarn over

Right shoulder

Finishing row

Attach yarn
Finishing row

Hold 18 sts.

5 sts

Finishing

Right shoulder

① Row 1:
Purl 47 sts, leaving 5 sts on left needle.

━ 47 sts ━

② Row 2 (first row of neck edge):
Turn to right side.

Knit (11 sts)

Yarn over needle, slip first st of left needle onto right needle and knit next 11 sts.

Yarn over.

③ Second row has been worked.

④ Row 3:
Bind off 2 sts at neck edge.

Slip first st, purl 1, pass slipped st over purl st.

Purl 3rd st and pass 2nd st over 3rd st.

⑤ Third row has been worked.

Five more sts are left on left needle.

Two sts have been bound off.

Neck edge

⑥ Fourth row has been worked (third row of neck edge).
Turn to right side and work as for step ②. Neck edge

Knit

Slipped st.
Yarn over.

Purl 2 sts tog.

⑦ Finishing Row:

Change position of slipped st and next st.

Neck edge

⑧ Finishing row has been worked.

Neck edge

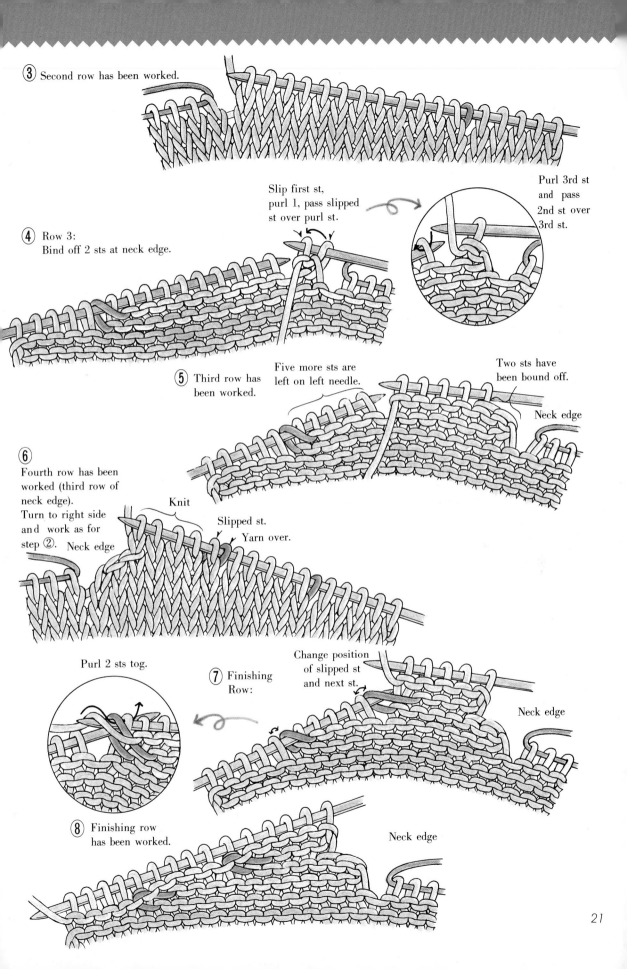

Left shoulder ① Row 2 (first row of neck edge):

Leave 5 sts
on left needle.

Attach yarn.

Neck edge

18 sts

Row 3 (second row of neck edge): Turn.

Yarn over and slip first
st onto right needle.

Yarn over

Neck edge

③ Third row has been worked.

Neck edge

Slip first st onto left needle, knit next
st and pass slipped st over knit st.

Neck
edge

④ Row 4: Bind off
2 sts at neck edge.

Two sts have
been bound off.

Neck
edge

⑤ Fourth row has
been worked.

Neck
edge

⑥ Fifth row has been worked.
Turn to wrong
side and work as
for step ②.

Neck
edge

Knit 2
sts tog.

2 sts tog.

Neck
edge

⑦ Finishing Row.

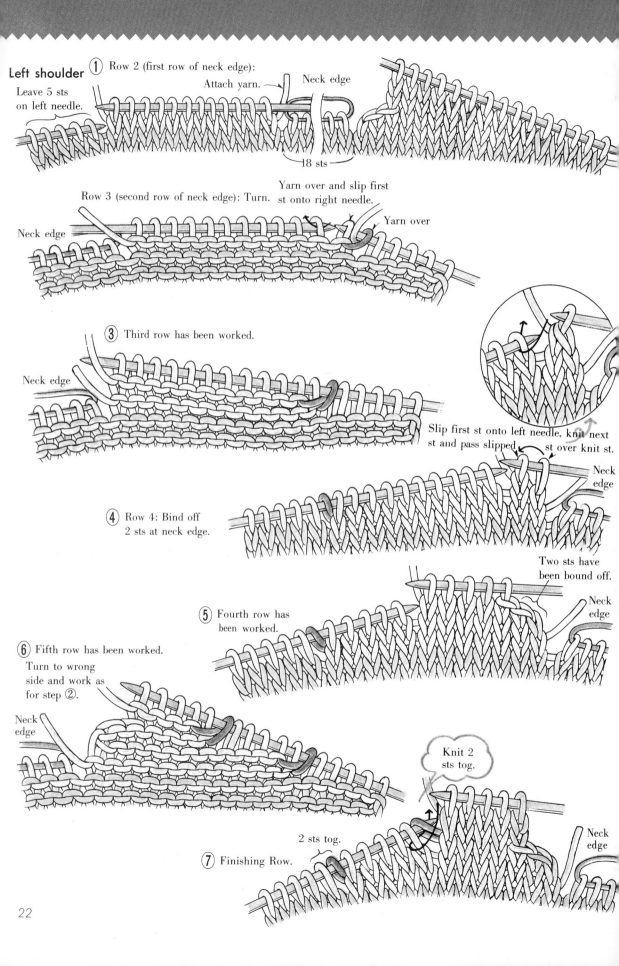

Shaping wedged edge:

This method is often used for forming bottom of vest, sweater or rompers.

⊂⊃ = Yarn over

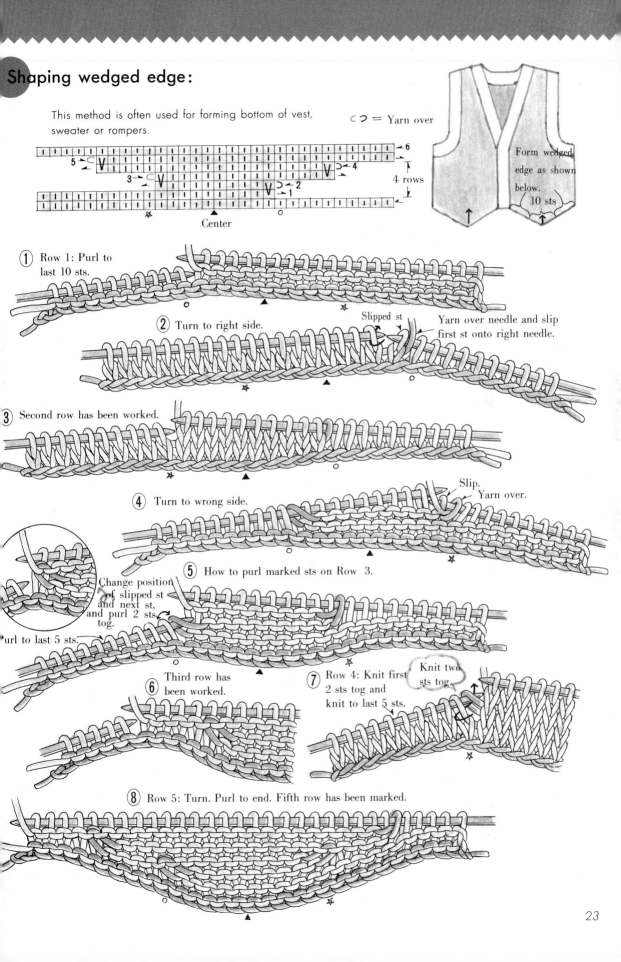

Form wedged edge as shown below.

10 sts

4 rows

Center

① Row 1: Purl to last 10 sts.

② Turn to right side.

Slipped st

Yarn over needle and slip first st onto right needle.

③ Second row has been worked.

④ Turn to wrong side.

Slip.
Yarn over.

⑤ How to purl marked sts on Row 3.

Change position of slipped st and next st, and purl 2 sts tog.

Purl to last 5 sts.

⑥ Third row has been worked.

⑦ Row 4: Knit first 2 sts tog and knit to last 5 sts.

Knit two sts tog.

⑧ Row 5: Turn. Purl to end. Fifth row has been marked.

23

Fastening

Binding off:

This method is often used for finishing off. The length of yarn to be used for binding off is 4–5 times as long as the width of edge to be bound off.

Binding off using knitting needles

Use knitting needles when binding off several stitches in the course of knitting to make buttonholes, pocket or to shape armholes and so on.

Binding off in stockinette st with knit side facing

① Knit first 2 sts and pass first st over second st. ② Knit third st and pass second st over. ③

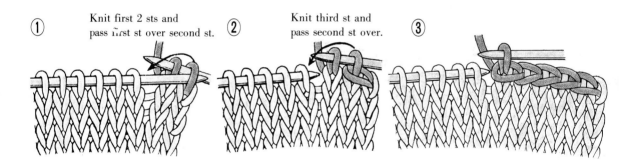

Binding off in reverse stockinette st with purl side facing

① Purl first 2 sts and pass first st over second st. ② Purl 3rd st and pass 2nd st over. ③

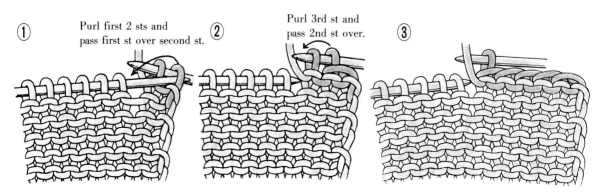

Binding off using crochet hook.

Crochet hook is used for binding off many stitches at a time.

Binding off in stockinette st with knit side facing

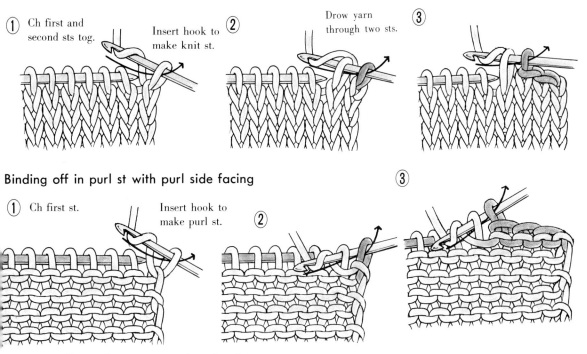

① Ch first and second sts tog. Insert hook to make knit st. ② Drow yarn through two sts. ③

Binding off in purl st with purl side facing

① Ch first st. Insert hook to make purl st. ② ③

Binding off in rib using crochet hook.

When you use crochet hook for binding off in rib you can work faster and more easily.
Work for purl and knit alternately depending on the stitches to be bound off.

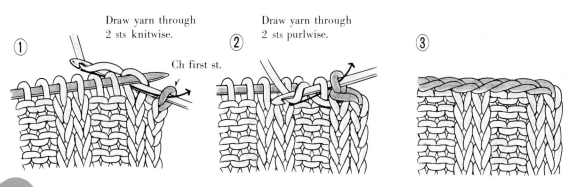

① Draw yarn through 2 sts knitwise. Ch first st. ② Draw yarn through 2 sts purlwise. ③

Fastening off in half-back stitch with tapestry needle:

Cut off yarn 3 times as long as the width of edge to be fastened off.
This method is suitable for fastening off in garter stitch or other edges requiring more elasticity.

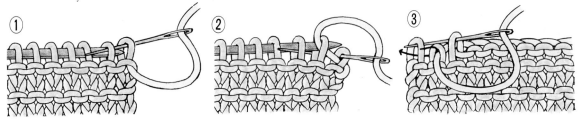

① ② ③

Fastening off in rib with tapestry needle

Ribbed edge is finished off in rib with tapestry needle as shown below. It may take time, but finished edge has elasticity and the same ribbing. Cut off yarn leaving a length 3–4 times the width of edge to be fastened off. Don't pull yarn too tight nor leave it too loose.

Fastening off in K1, P1 rib.:

For Flat Edge

With 2 knit sts at each end

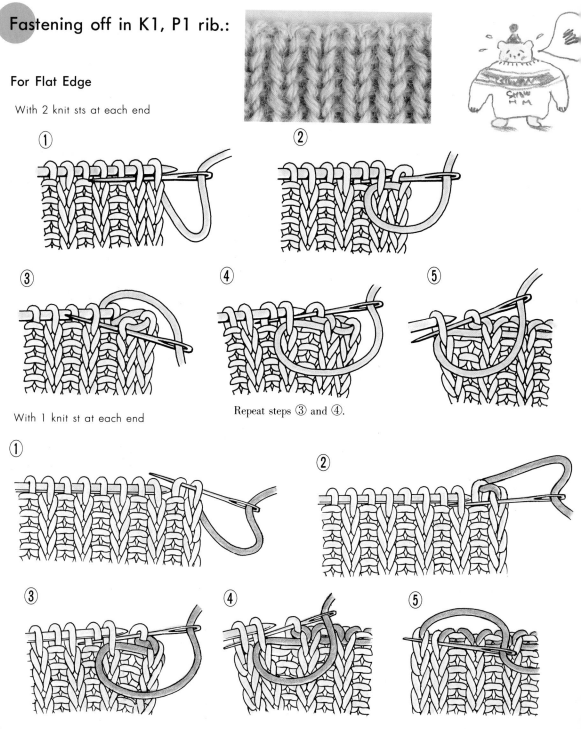

① ②

③ ④ ⑤

With 1 knit st at each end

Repeat steps ③ and ④.

① ②

③ ④ ⑤

Make all fastened-off stitches even

Insert needle into fastened-off stitches and make all stitches even by gently pulling knitting with left hand while holding needle with right hand.

For Circular Edge

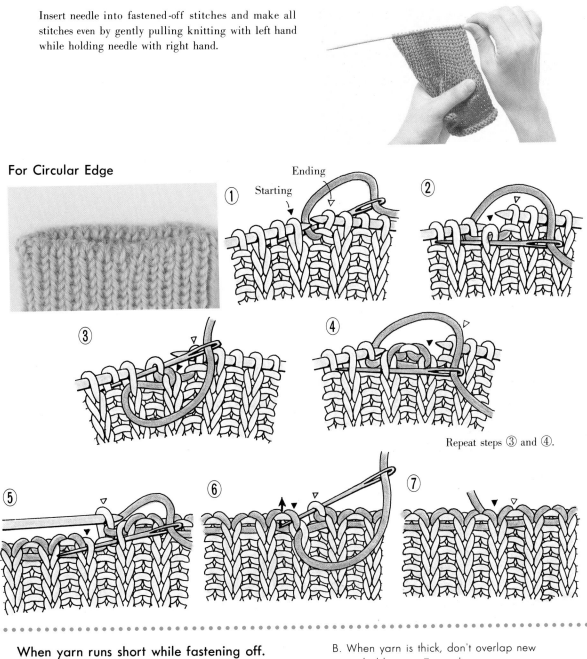

Repeat steps ③ and ④.

When yarn runs short while fastening off.

A. Insert needle with new yarn into last 2 sts already fastened off and work in same manner.

B. When yarn is thick, don't overlap new and old yarns. Tie ends.

Wrong side

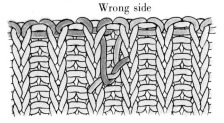

Fastening off in K2, P2 rib.:

For Flat Edge

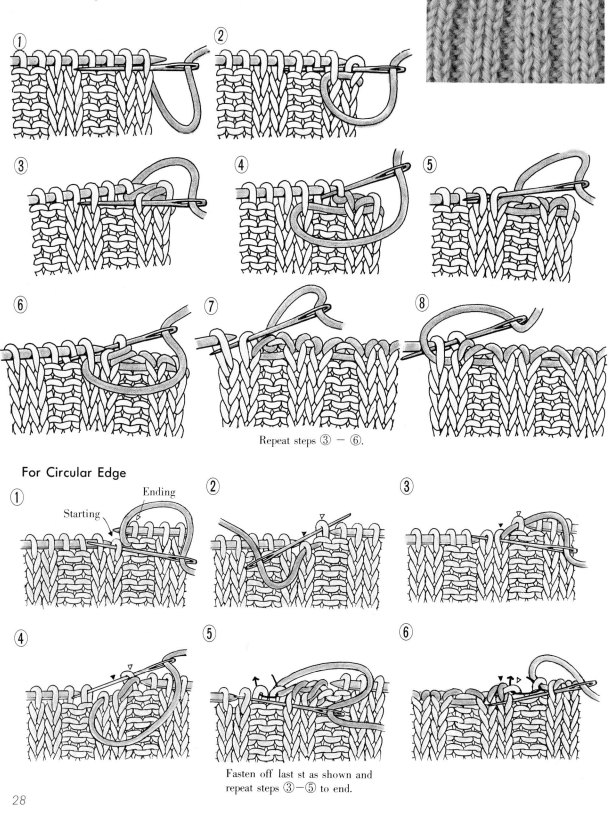

Repeat steps ③ — ⑥.

For Circular Edge

① Starting Ending

② ③

④ ⑤ ⑥

Fasten off last st as shown and
repeat steps ③—⑤ to end.

Grafting (Joining two pieces in same stitch)

Lay two pieces together so that edge stitches match and graft as shown below using tapestry needle. Grafting is done to make a row of the same stitches as the pieces to be joined. Cut off yarn leaving a length 3–4 times as long as the width of edge to be grafted.

Grafting in stockinette st.:

This method can be used for joining stitches kept on two needles, bound-off edge and stitches on one needle or bound-off edges.

Grafting stitches kept on two needles

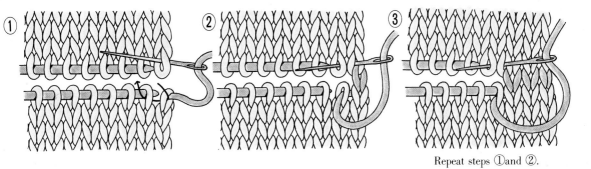

Repeat steps ①and ②.

Grafting bound-off edge and stitches kept on one needle.

Two pieces can be joined without showing seam and the seam does not stretch too much because one edge has been bound off.

Repeat steps ② and ③.

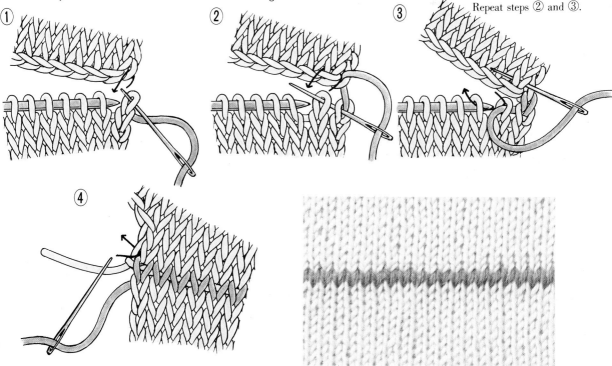

Grafting in reverse stockinette st:

Insert tapestry needle as shown to graft in reverse stockinette st.

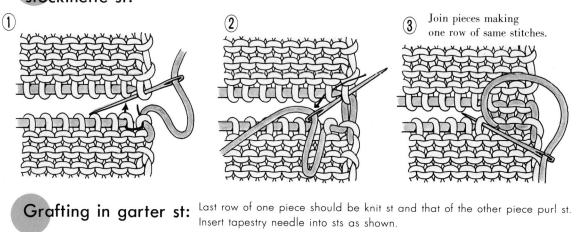

① ② ③ Join pieces making one row of same stitches.

Grafting in garter st:

Last row of one piece should be knit st and that of the other piece purl st. Insert tapestry needle into sts as shown.

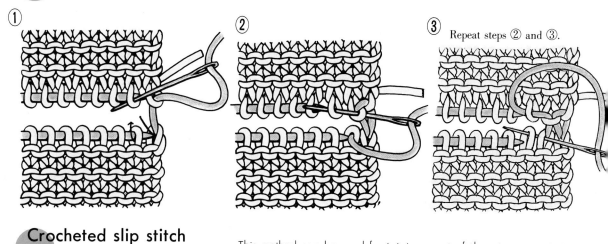

① ② ③ Repeat steps ② and ③.

Crocheted slip stitch variation:

This method can be used for joining most of the pieces, so it is worth learning. Slip stitch through opposite stitch and chain 2 sts together.

① Place two pieces with right sides facing. Pass first st through first st of second piece.

② Chain first st. Repeat step ①. → A

③ Yarn over and inse_ needle into 2 sts. → B

④ Repeat steps A and B.

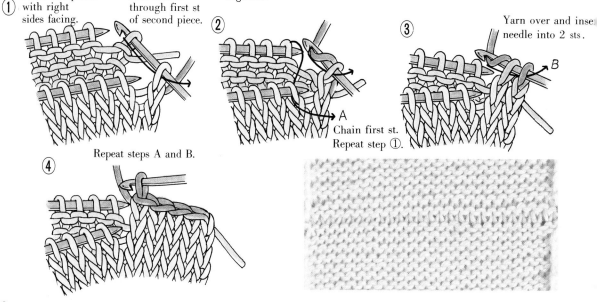

Crocheted slip stitch: It is easy to work and also to rip out. Keep even tension while working.

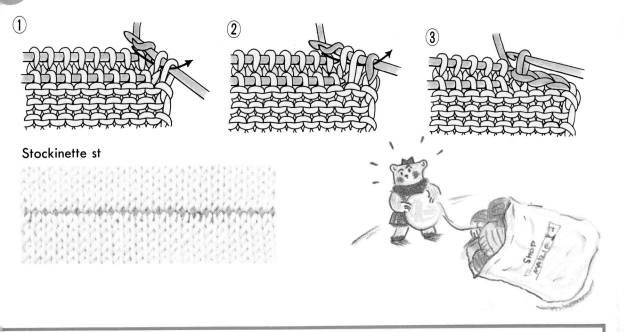

Stockinette st

Tension or Gauge

Tension or gauge refers to the number of stitches and rows to a given measurement (usually 10cm square). Each knitter works differently, so it is essential to make a sample square to get the right tension before starting.

● Sample square

Using yarn and needles to be used for the project, make a piece of knitting, 20cm square, in same stitch as the project. Block this and leave to dry. Follow directions written in the label for pressing synthetic yarn.

surement), change needles to larger size and if too loose, change them to smaller size.

● Check gauge

Smooth out the sample and place it on a flat surface. Count number of stitches and rows within center 10cm square. If your tension is too tight (that is, if you have more stitches and rows to the given mea-

Seams

Place edges to be joined side by side and work as shown below. Cut off yarn leaving 40cm–50cm length and thread end into tapestry needle. Insert needle between first and second sts on left edge and pass under one row. Insert needle between sts on right edge and pass under one row. Continue working from side to side matching rows.

Invisible seam   Joining side seam of K1, P1 rib.:

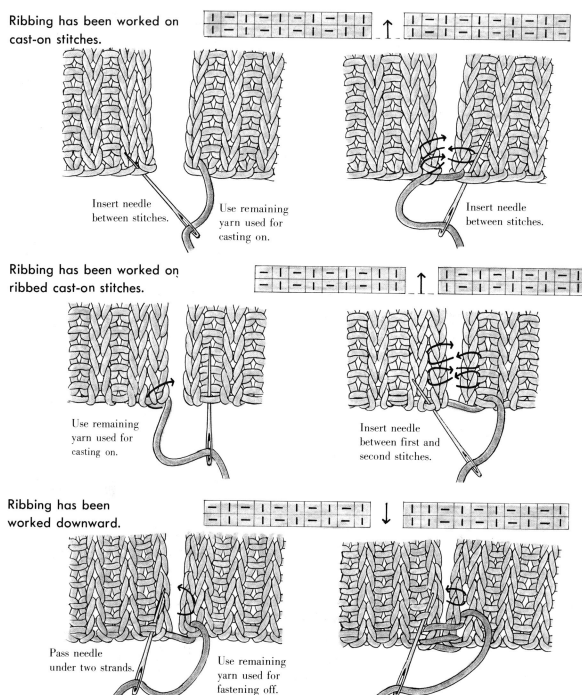

Ribbing has been worked on cast-on stitches.

Insert needle between stitches.

Use remaining yarn used for casting on.

Insert needle between stitches.

Ribbing has been worked on ribbed cast-on stitches.

Use remaining yarn used for casting on.

Insert needle between first and second stitches.

Ribbing has been worked downward.

Pass needle under two strands.

Use remaining yarn used for fastening off.

Side seams, underarm and ribbed edges

Always leave a 40–50cm long end of yarn when starting or ending for later use. Start seam from bottom edges which are usually worked in ribbing.

When ribbing has been worked downward, join as shown.

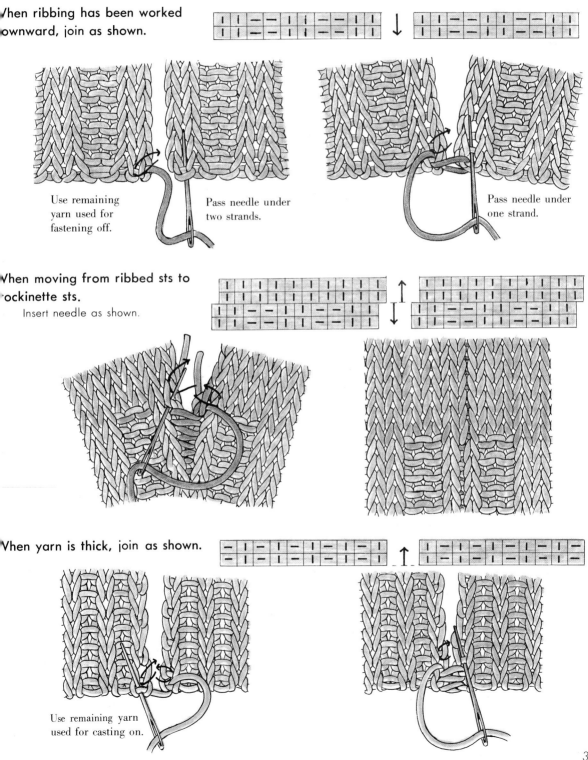

Use remaining
yarn used for
fastening off.

Pass needle under
two strands.

Pass needle under
one strand.

When moving from ribbed sts to stockinette sts.

Insert needle as shown.

When yarn is thick, join as shown.

Use remaining yarn
used for casting on.

Joining edges of stockinette st

Insert needle between first and second stitches and join as shown.

Joining edges of increased stitches

Insert needle as shown.

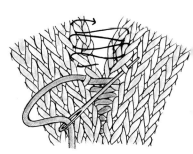

Joining edges of reverse stockinette stitches

Place pieces side by side with right side up. Insert needle as shown, pass under two rows of left side, then under one row of right side and one row of left side alternately.

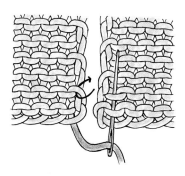

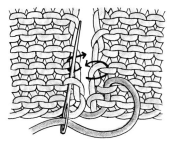

Joining edges of garter stitches:

Insert needle and join as shown.

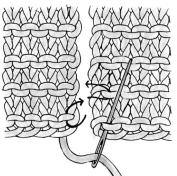

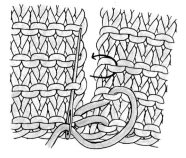

Flat seam:

When joining back of sock or edges of babywear which need flat seam, this method is suitable. Place edges side by side and insert needle as shown.

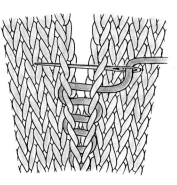

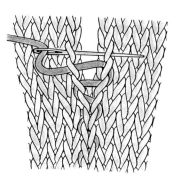

Joining raglan sleeve to body

With right sides facing, join sleeve and body with crocheted slip stitch. Then turn to right side and join as shown using tapestry needle.

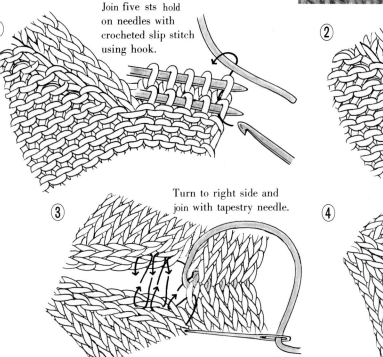

① Join five sts hold on needles with crocheted slip stitch using hook.

② After joining 5 sts, drop hook and pull yarn through last loop.

③ Turn to right side and join with tapestry needle.

④

Joining turn-over edge (neck, bottom and sleeve edges)

·afting method Knit first row of turn-over edge with thread in contrasting color to mark grafting line. This method is suitable for joining neck edge or edges which need elasticity.

·ining in slip stitch

This method is suitable when yarn is not smooth.
Split yarn into 1 or 2 plies when yarn is thick.

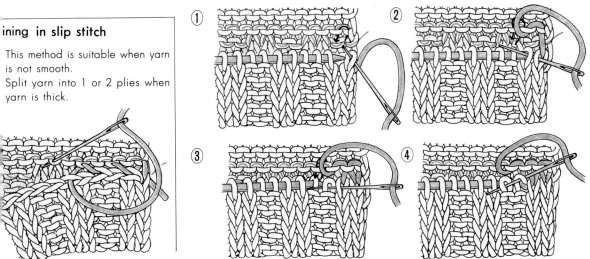

① ② ③ ④

Knitting Colors

To change colors, carry yarn across back of work and twist one color with another or cut off one color and attach another depending on the design. For isolated design or Argyle pattern, cut off yarn each time you change colors. For allover design, carry yarn across back of work. The key to knitting colors depends on carrying yarn properly. Don't carry yarn too loosely nor too tight.

Carrying yarn across back of work :

Carry the color not in use loosely across back of work. Always carry background color below pattern color without twisting.

Chart for Knitting Colors

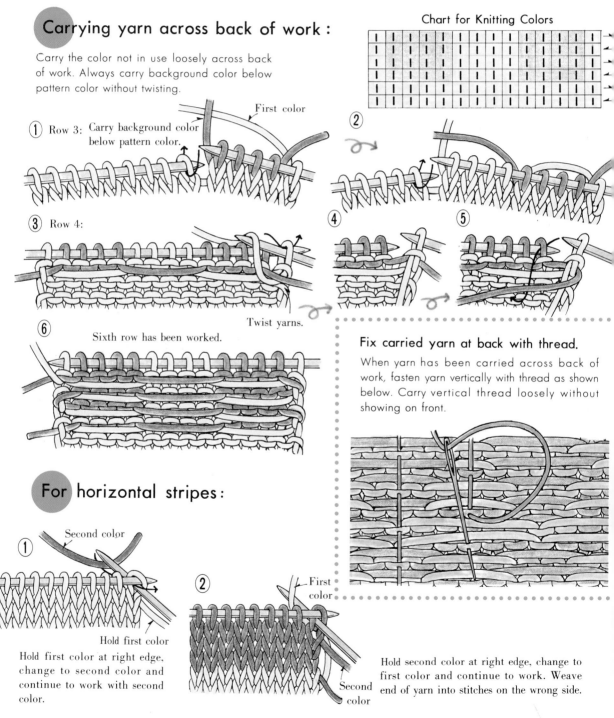

① Row 3: Carry background color below pattern color.

First color

②

③ Row 4:

④

⑤

Twist yarns.

⑥ Sixth row has been worked.

Fix carried yarn at back with thread.

When yarn has been carried across back of work, fasten yarn vertically with thread as shown below. Carry vertical thread loosely without showing on front.

For horizontal stripes :

① Second color

Hold first color

Hold first color at right edge, change to second color and continue to work with second color.

② First color

Second color

Hold second color at right edge, change to first color and continue to work. Weave end of yarn into stitches on the wrong side.

36

For isolated design:

Join pattern color each time to make design and cut off when finished. Twist pattern and background colors when changing colors to avoid making holes.

□ = Background color
▨ = Pattern color

① Row 1:
Join pattern color for design.
Background color

② Row 2:

③ Row 3:
Twist pattern color around background color.

④ Row 5:
Twist.

⑤ Row 8:

For vertical stripes:

①
Pattern color — Twist.
Twist pattern and background colors to avoid making holes.

②
Twist yarns whenever changing colors.

③
Twist.
Wrong side

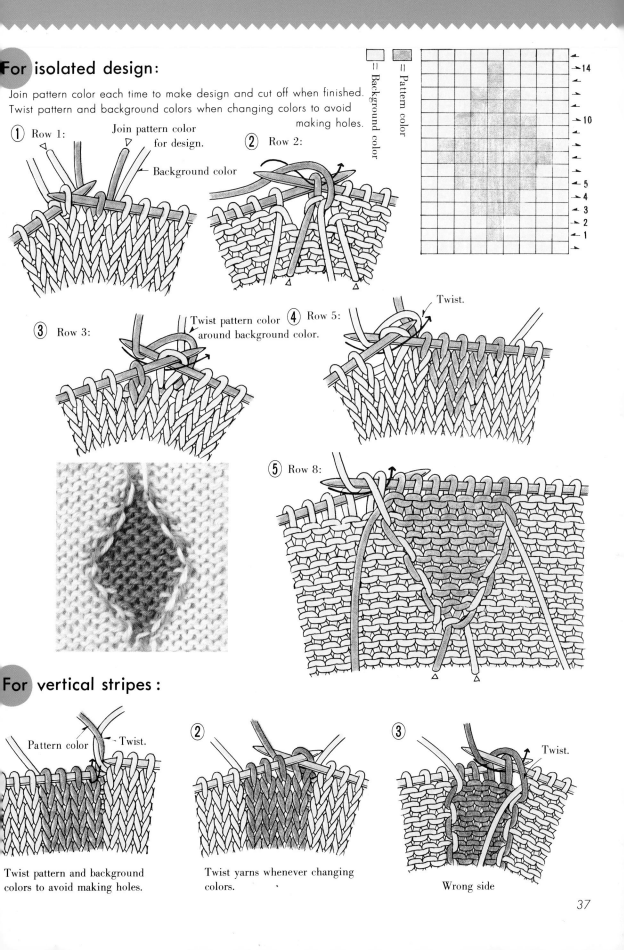

Sewing in Sleeves

Sleeves are often made separately and are sewn onto body.
Sometimes stitches are picked up around armholes and sleeves are made.
To sew in sleeves, crocheted slip stitch or half back stitch is used.

1. Divide armhole and sleeve edge equally and mark.

Divide front armhole into thirds equally and mark
with contrasting color. Divide and mark back armhole
in the same way.

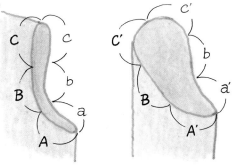

2. Match marks and pin body and sleeve together.

With right sides facing pin body and sleeve together matching marks and easing sleeve cap.

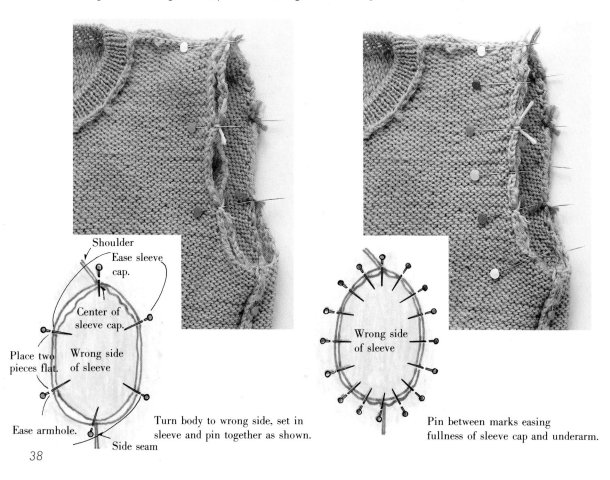

Shoulder
Ease sleeve cap.

Center of sleeve cap.

Place two pieces flat.

Wrong side of sleeve

Ease armhole.

Side seam

Turn body to wrong side, set in
sleeve and pin together as shown.

Wrong side of sleeve

Pin between marks easing
fullness of sleeve cap and underarm.

Start sewing or crocheting from underarm.

Using yarn in same color (always use straight yarn for sewing), sew body and sleeve together with even tension inserting needle into one stitch (or one and half stitches) in from edge at right angles.

Half back stitch:

With right sides facing, insert needle through two layers, one stitch in from the edge, and sew in half back stitch. Pull thread tight after each stitch.

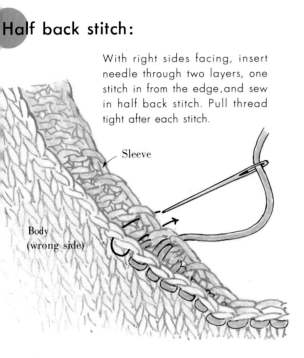

Crocheted slip stitch:

With right sides facing, start working at side seam in crocheted slip stitch with hook.
Insert hook through two layers at right angles.

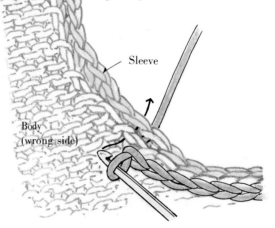

Work single crochet along sleeve cap.

Work single crochet along sleeve cap with tight tension to secure seam. Then, steam-press. Seams will turn to sleeve side.

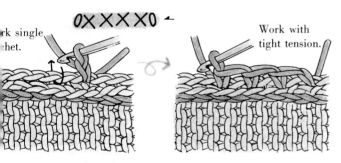

Crocheted slip stitch.

Single crochet has been worked over seams of sleeve cap.

Making Buttonholes

Making buttonholes while working:

For small hole: Yarn over needle once and knit next 2 sts together.

① Knit 2 sts tog.
3rd row
Yarn over

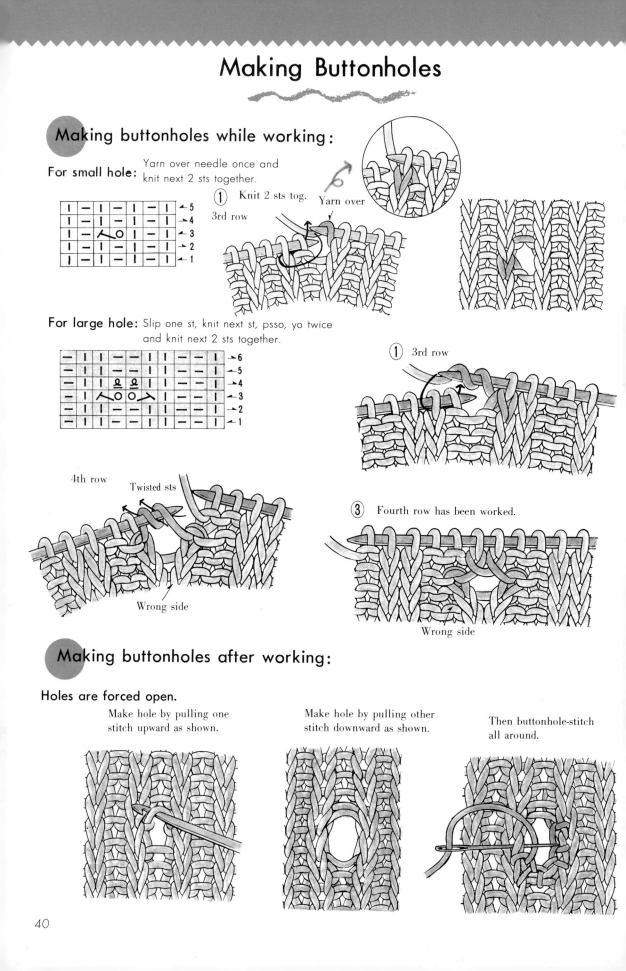

For large hole:
Slip one st, knit next st, psso, yo twice and knit next 2 sts together.

① 3rd row

4th row
Twisted sts
Wrong side

③ Fourth row has been worked.
Wrong side

Making buttonholes after working:

Holes are forced open.

Make hole by pulling one stitch upward as shown.

Make hole by pulling other stitch downward as shown.

Then buttonhole-stitch all around.